MOTHER'S
JOURNEY

*A Devotional **for Pregnancy***

MOTHER'S
JOURNEY

*A Devotional **for Pregnancy***

MELISSA HEILAND

HENDRICKSON PUBLISHERS

A Mother's Journey: A Devotional for Pregnancy

© 2011 Hendrickson Publishers Marketing, LLC
P. O. Box 3473
Peabody, Massachusetts 01961-3473
www.hendrickson.com

ISBN 978-1-61970-496-1

Scripture references are taken from the Holy Bible, New International Version®, NIV®. Copyright © 1973, 1978, 1984, 2011 by Biblica, Inc.™ Used by permission of Zondervan. All rights reserved worldwide. www.zondervan.com The "NIV" and "New International Version" are trademarks registered in the United States Patent and Trademark Office by Biblica, Inc.™

All references to baby development are excerpted from *The First Nine Months*, a Focus on the Family publication. Copyright © 1999–2010, Focus on the Family. Used by permission.

For more information, please contact:

Melissa Heiland
mheiland@comcast.net
www.beautifulfeetinternational.com

Printed in the United States of America

Third Hendrickson Edition Printing — February 2019

This book is dedicated to my friend and brother in Christ, Todd Metts. You lived and died serving God. We will be praising God together again one day in heaven.

Acknowledgments

I first of all must thank my Lord and Savior Jesus Christ. He gives me life, sustains my life and everything good in my life is because of him.

Secondly, thanks go to my husband, Ken. He has always shown me what Jesus is like—loving, forgiving, faithful, patient. I would not have written this book without his unending encouragement and support.

Thank you to my children—Michael, Josh, Melissa, Jack, Andy, and Nick. I love you more than you know. I pray God will bless you beyond your wildest dreams.

I am very grateful to Focus on the Family for their help in putting together this book. Thanks especially to Betsy Powell for her generous contribution.

Thank you to my praying friends. Your partnership is invaluable to me. This book is a result of your work on your knees.

Thank you to all of my sisters in pregnancy care ministry. Your love, support, encouragement, and wisdom is a continual blessing.

Special thanks to Cindy Johanson, executive director of the Central Florida Pregnancy Center. God created us alike and brought us together for his service, and I am grateful for that.

Thanks to my sister, friend, and co-laborer, Mary Margaret Gibson. Your encouragement and support are more significant than you know.

Dear Friend . . .

I know that your mind is racing with thoughts and fears. I have sat with hundreds of women over the past two decades as they found out that they were pregnant. I know that every situation is unique. No one has ever experienced exactly what you are dealing with in your life right now. You have circumstances that may be extremely difficult. I want you to know that you are not alone. There are people who want to help you and a God who cares. I have written this book to provide a source of comfort, hope, and inspiration to you. It is my joy and privilege to sit and listen to women as they seek to decide what is best for their babies and themselves. Thank you for letting me talk to you through this book. I pray that God will use it to encourage you and to help you as you work to put things into perspective and make decisions that are best for you. You are precious.

Love and prayers,
Melissa

4 WEEKS: A pregnancy test taken at this point can measure hCG, the pregnancy hormone in the mother's urine, and tell her if she is pregnant. By now, the embryo is completely attached to the lining of the uterus and draws nourishment from its mother.

Streams in the Desert

Read Isaiah 43:18–21

"See, I am doing a new thing! Now it springs up; do you not perceive it? I am making a way in the desert and streams in the wasteland." (v. 19)

You just received news that will change your life. You are pregnant. You may be happy or sad or confused. You are probably scared. You have so many questions and too few answers. This may be a surprise to you, but one thing is certain. This is not a surprise to God. God knows this baby, and he knows you. He knows all of your questions, and he knows all of the answers. He has a plan for you, and he is doing a new thing in your body even now. Although the road ahead of you may look difficult or even impossible, that's not true. God is doing something new and different in your life, and he will make a way in the desert for you. Nothing is impossible for God. This is why he says he will make streams in the wasteland. Take a deep breath and listen to his voice as he tells you that he is doing something new and good for you. He will make a way for you. He loves you.

Father, I have so many emotions inside of me. Thank you for understanding me and hearing my prayers. You know my situation and what I need for today and for the days to come. Please take care of me and help me to do the things you want me to do. Thank you for making a way in the desert for me. Amen.

Write down your feelings. List all the exciting possibilities and some things that worry you. Trust God with all of it.

5 **WEEKS:** The heart begins to beat just twenty-one days after fertilization, or five weeks after the mother's last menstrual period began. The heart, about the size of a poppy seed, is the first organ to function. The first signs of brain development are evident, and the foundation for every organ system is already established and beginning to develop.

In His Image

Read Genesis 1:1–2:2

So God created man in his own image, in the image of God he created him; male and female he created them. (v. 27)

This is the story of God creating the whole world. God made wonderful things: the sun to keep us warm and the moon to light the night, flowers for beauty and fragrance, puppies to love us and stars to fill the sky. His saved his most beautiful and wonderful creation of all for last. He created us his children in his image. This means that we are very special to God. He created us to know him and to love him and to be loved by him. He has created that very small person who is living inside of you now. The God who created the whole world is the same God who made you and who made the baby that is in your womb right now. God said that everything he made was very good. He is doing something amazing inside of your body now.

Dear God, thank you for making this beautiful world, and thank you for making me. Thank you also for this baby that is inside of me now. I pray that you will help me as I make decisions each day. In Jesus' name, amen.

Write about what you think it means to be made in God's image.
List the ways that God has made you that are very good.

6 **WEEKS:** Just four weeks after fertilization, the baby is growing rapidly and measures one-eighth of an inch long. The basic structure for the entire central nervous system (brain and spinal cord) has formed. The eyes are developing, and the arm and leg buds are now visible. The beating heart can be seen on an ultrasound scan—it's already beating 100 to 120 times a minute!

Rainbows in the Clouds

Read Genesis 9:7–17

"Whenever the rainbow appears in the clouds, I will see it and remember the everlasting covenant between God and all the living creatures of every kind on the earth." (v. 16)

You may have heard the story of Noah. Noah lived on earth during a time when people were wicked and very rebellious against God. In fact, people were so wicked that the Lord decided to destroy the earth and begin again. He would begin again with Noah, who was a righteous man. The Bible tells us that Noah walked with God; he loved and obeyed God. So the Lord told Noah to build a boat and to put two of every kind of animal, one male and one female, on the boat, along with his wife and sons and their wives. Then the Lord sent a great flood to destroy the earth. Only those on the ark survived. After it rained for forty days and nights and the water had receded, God told Noah to come out of the boat with his family and the animals and to repopulate the earth. He promised that he would never again destroy the whole earth with a flood, and he put a rainbow in the sky as a reminder of this promise.

A rainbow is a sign of hope. It shows us that after the storms of life there is hope for the future. There is hope for you and your future, no matter what trials you may be facing now. Look to the sky for rainbows and for the One who made them. He will take care of you.

Dear God, I thank you for the hope I have in you. Please show me rainbows. Amen.

Write about the things that concern you now and about your hopes for the future.

7 **WEEKS:** The baby is now one-third of an inch long. The embryo makes its own blood. Depending on the baby's gender, the testicles or ovaries are beginning to form.

The God Who Sees Me

Read Genesis 16:1–13

She gave this name to the Lord who spoke to her: "You are the God who sees me," for she said, "I have now seen the One who sees me." (v. 13)

God had chosen Abram to be the father of his chosen people, the nation of Israel. Abram and his wife, Sarai, were old and had no children. God had promised them that they would have many children, but because Sarai had not gotten pregnant, she came up with a plan. She gave her servant, Hagar, to her husband so that they could sleep together and have a child together. When Hagar became pregnant after doing what she was told, Sarai became angry with her and abused her, so Hagar ran away. She was alone and pregnant in the desert with no one to help her. The angel of the Lord came to her in the desert and told her that the Lord saw her pain and would give her a son. She named God "the God who sees me."

This same God who saw Hagar alone and afraid in the desert sees you. He knows what you have been through, and he knows what you need. Trust him to help you now.

Dear God, I thank you that you see me and that you love me. Please help me through this time in my life. Amen.

Write a prayer to God telling him what you are dealing with and asking him to guide you in your next steps.

WEEK 8

8 **WEEKS:** At eight weeks, the embryo can respond to touch by reflex. The baby is now about half an inch long. The elbows and fingers can be seen. Some reports show that the embryo can move its trunk and limbs. Lungs begin to develop, taste buds are forming on the tongue, tooth buds for "baby teeth" are taking shape in the jaw, and eyelids are beginning to form.

A Pregnant Virgin?

Read Luke 1:1–38

"For nothing is impossible with God." (v. 37, NLT)

Mary was a teenager who had never slept with a man. One day an angel came to her and told her that she was going to give birth to a baby boy and that this boy would save the world. She was confused and asked how this could happen. The angel told her that everything was possible with God. Although she was scared and confused, she submitted to God's plan for her life. She would have to face many difficult things beginning with explaining to her parents and her fiancé that she was pregnant. But she was willing to obey in spite of the cost.

You too may be shocked that you are pregnant. Your baby is not a surprise to God. You can be sure that he has a plan for you and your baby.

Dear God, I want to be like Mary. I want to obey you. Thank you for giving me this baby. Help me to take care of this child. Amen.

Write about your feelings about being pregnant. What is the most difficult part? What are you excited about?

9 **WEEKS:** The baby measures three-fourths of an inch long and weighs almost one-eighth of an ounce. The developing ears and nose are visible, and there is pigment in the retina. Nipples can now be seen on the chest. The limbs and fingers are growing rapidly, and the bones in the arms are beginning to calcify and harden.

God Sent His Son

Read John 3:1–17

For God so loved the world that he gave his one and only Son, that whoever believes in him shall not perish but have eternal life. (v. 16)

A man named Nicodemus, who was a member of the Jewish ruling council, came to Jesus asking him questions about eternal life. Jesus told him that he had to be born again to get to heaven. This didn't make any sense to Nicodemus. He knew he could not return to his mother's womb and be re-born. Jesus went on to explain that he was talking about spiritual life. He explained that God had sent his Son, Jesus, to save the world, and the only way to God was to trust in Jesus for salvation. Jesus died in our place, to take the punishment for all the things we have done wrong. The Bible says we have fallen short of the glory of God. We do things that are not pleasing to God, and this separates us from him. But Jesus, God's perfect Son, came to earth to die in our place so that we could have eternal life. He died on the cross and rose again. The way to heaven is through faith in Jesus Christ. Would you trust him today?

Dear God, I know that I have sinned and that I need you. I believe that Jesus died on the cross for me and that he rose again. I trust in Jesus. Help me to follow him in my life. Thank you for saving me. Amen.

Write a prayer to God thanking him for all he has done for you.

10 **WEEKS:** The baby's brain is growing rapidly. Each minute it produces almost 250,000 new neurons! The upper and lower portions of the arms and legs are clearly seen, as well as the fingers and toes. By now the external ear is fully developed. A baby boy begins to produce the male hormone, testosterone.

The Lord Will Fight for You

Read Exodus 14:13–31

"The Lord will fight for you; you need only to be still." (v. 14)

God's people, the Israelites, had been enslaved by the Egyptians. The Lord sent Moses to release his people from captivity. As the Israelites fled, the Egyptian army pursued them and the Israelites were terrified. Moses told them not to be afraid but to watch for the deliverance the Lord would bring them. While they were being chased by the army, they came upon a great ocean, the Red Sea. Moses stretched out his hand over the sea and the waters parted. God's people went through the sea on dry ground, with a wall of water on their right and on their left. The Egyptian army came after them, but Moses again stretched out his hand and the sea went back to its place, drowning the Egyptian army.

You may feel overwhelmed with your circumstances right now. You may feel like the Israelites did when they faced an army behind them and a sea in front of them. You may also feel trapped, with nowhere to run. God has the same message for you that he had for the Israelites—"Be still, I will fight for you." Trust him to part the sea for you.

> Dear Lord, you know the circumstances in my life. I need you to make a path for me. Thank you for caring for me. Amen.

Tell the Lord what you need in your life. Ask him to make a way for you.

11 **WEEKS:** Because the baby has all of the major organ systems and is a distinctly recognizable human being, he or she is no longer called an embryo, but is now known as a fetus, a Latin word for "young one." The baby is about two inches long and can yawn and suck. The eyelids are fully formed and closed to protect the developing eyes. The kidneys begin to produce urine. During the next several weeks, his or her body will grow rapidly, increasing in weight thirty times and tripling in length!

A Mother's Care

Read Exodus 2:1–10

When the child grew older, she took him to Pharaoh's daughter and he became her son. She named him Moses, saying, "I drew him out of the water." (v. 10)

Moses was born to a Hebrew woman at a time when Pharaoh had made a law that all Hebrew baby boys must be killed. Moses' mother loved him, and so she hid him in a basket along the banks of the Nile River. Pharaoh's daughter found him and brought him home and raised him as her son. Moses' mother loved him so much that she allowed someone else to raise him because she knew that would be best.

You may be in a similar circumstance. Perhaps, like Moses' mother, you don't feel equipped to raise your child. You love your child so much that you will make an adoption plan for the little one God has given to you. Only brave and loving women do that for their children.

When Moses grew up, God used him in great ways. God will do the same with your child if you choose this path as well.

Lord, you know what is best for this child you have given me. Thank you for my child's life. Help me to know what is best for my baby. In Jesus' name, amen.

Write about your dreams for your child.

Hiding the Spies

Read Joshua 2

*"When we heard of it, our hearts melted and everyone's
courage failed because of you, for the LORD your God is
God in heaven above and on the earth below." (v. 11)*

The Lord had promised the Israelites that he would give them
a certain area of land called Jericho. So Joshua, Israel's leader after
Moses, sent spies into the land to learn about the best way to con-
quer it. They entered into the house of a prostitute named Rahab.
When the king of Jericho ordered Rahab to send out the spies,
she hid them and told the king that she did not know where they
had gone. Rahab knew that the spies were sent from God, and so
she protected them. They, in turn, protected her and her family
when they later conquered the land God had given to them.

Like Rahab, we all have things in our lives that we are not
proud of, areas where we have failed God and others. With God,
there is always second chance, an opportunity to turn from doing
wrong things and begin to follow God's plan for our lives. Is there
anything you need to change today?

> Dear God, I know that you are a loving and forgiving God. I
> know there are things in my life that don't please you, but
> that you still can use me to help others. Show me what you
> want me to do. I love you. Amen.

List ways that God can use you to help others.

Victory

Read Joshua 5:13–6:24

Then Joshua fell facedown to the ground in reverence, and asked him, "What message does my Lord have for his servant?" (5:14)

Joshua was preparing to overtake Jericho because God had told him that the land was his to take. The Lord sent an angel to Joshua as he was getting ready to go to battle. Immediately, Joshua fell to the ground and asked for instructions from the Lord. The angel brought strange instructions to this warrior. He told him to march once around the city each day for six days and on the seventh day to march around the city seven times, blowing trumpets and shouting. This must have sounded very strange to a man who was trained in battle. But Joshua obeyed, and the walls of the city fell down without any battle. The city was destroyed, and only Rahab the prostitute and her family were saved.

This is a great example for us. We must be ready to ask God what he wants us to do in our lives, and we must be willing to obey what he tells us.

> Father God, show me what you want me to do for myself and for my child. Reveal your will to me. I want to obey. In Jesus' name, amen.

Write a prayer to God asking him what he wants you to do to take care of yourself and your baby. Write about your goals and dreams for yourself and your child.

14 **WEEKS:** Now 3½ inches long, the "young one" is coordinated enough to find his or her thumb and suck it. Fingernails and toenails are beginning to grow. The baby is also able to swallow and urinate.

A Real-Life Fairy Tale

Read Esther 2:1–15

When the turn came for Esther (the young woman Mordecai had adopted, the daughter of his uncle Abihail) to go to the king, she asked for nothing other than what Hegai, the king's eunuch who was in charge of the harem, suggested. And Esther won the favor of everyone who saw her. (v. 15)

Esther was an ordinary girl who was orphaned as a child. Her uncle adopted her, and when the king was looking for a queen, he encouraged her to apply for the job. Esther was chosen from all the contestants, and God used her eventually to save all the Jews from death. An evil man had plans to kill all of the Jews, but God used Esther, the Jewish queen, to save his people.

I'm sure Esther never imagined that she could be queen or that God would use her to save his people. You may never be queen, but God has great plans for your life as well. God uses ordinary people throughout the Bible to change the world. You can be sure that he has amazing plans for you too. Nothing is impossible with God.

Father, I thank you for this incredible story of Esther. I believe that you can do extraordinary things in my life and in the life of my child too. Amen.

Write about your dreams for yourself and your child. Wait with excitement to see what God will do.

Meat at Twilight

Read Exodus 16:1–18

*"I have heard the grumbling of the Israelites, Tell them, 'At twilight you will eat meat, and in the morning you will be filled with bread. Then you will know that I am the L*ORD *your God.'"* (v. 12)

After the Lord delivered the Israelites from slavery in an amazing way by parting the Red Sea, the Israelites started to grumble and complain. They were traveling across the desert, and they were hungry. They missed the food they had eaten when they were captives. The Lord heard their complaining, and he again provided for them. He sent bread from heaven for them every morning and quail for them to eat each night.

Even though the Israelites were ungrateful, God still took care of them and gave them what they asked for. God will take care of you too. Tell him what you need.

Dear God, I don't want to be ungrateful like the Israelites. I know you have taken care of me many times in the past. I need you now. Amen.

Begin by thanking God for your baby and all of his gifts. Then make a list of your needs, expecting God to hear you.

16 **WEEKS:** The heart beats between 110 and 180 times per minute and pumps about twenty-six gallons of blood each day. The gender of the baby might be seen on ultrasound. If she is a girl, millions of eggs are now forming in her ovaries. At almost five inches in length and weighing nearly four ounces, the baby can coordinate the movement of its arms and legs, though his or her mother will not likely feel it yet.

Do Not Be Distressed

Read Genesis 45:1–15

"And now, do not be distressed and do not be angry with yourselves for selling me here, because it was to save lives that God sent me ahead of you." (v. 5)

Joseph was the youngest son in his family, and his father loved him best. This caused his older brothers to be jealous, so jealous that they sold him into slavery. He later became a trusted advisor to the ruler of the land, Pharaoh. He became the second most important person in the country of Egypt. Many years later, a famine came to the land and the older brothers went to Egypt to try to buy grain for their family so they would not starve. They had to go before their brother Joseph to ask for food. They did not recognize him as the brother they had sold into slavery many years before, but he knew who they were. When he told them he was their baby brother, he also forgave them for the terrible thing they had done to him when he was younger. He told them that God had sent him to Egypt ahead of them so that he would be able to take care of them. He forgave them, and he helped them even though they had been cruel to him. Joseph trusted that God would take care of him even when people would not. He trusted God to bring good things out of bad situations. You can too.

Father, I thank you that I can trust you. Help me to forgive those who have hurt me. Help me to learn to trust you in all situations, even when I don't understand. Amen

Is there anyone you need to forgive? Write a prayer asking God to help you forgive and trust him to work things out.

Perfectly Cared For

Read Psalm 23

The LORD is my shepherd, I lack nothing.
He makes me lie down in green pastures,
he leads me beside quiet waters,
he refreshes my soul. (vv. 1–3)

Sheep are helpless without a shepherd. The shepherd brings them to food and water. Without the shepherd, they eat things that will kill them and drink water that makes them sick. They get lost very easily because they have no sense of direction. Because of their body shape, when they fall down they can't get up without help. Without the shepherd, they will starve to death. Sometimes the shepherd must risk his life to protect the sheep from danger.

In many ways we are like sheep. We make choices that hurt us. We can't seem to figure out where to go and what to do on our own. Jesus calls Himself "The Good Shepherd." He was willing to die to take care of us, his sheep. When we stay close to our shepherd, we are safe and have nothing to fear.

Dear God, Thank you for taking care of me and my baby. Help me to stay close to you. Amen.

What are some dangers you see in your life? How can you avoid making dangerous choices?

18 **WEEKS:** In just two weeks, the fetus has almost doubled its weight to seven ounces. The skeleton is hardening and calcifying and is visible on ultrasound. Reflexes such as blinking and frowning are now developed. The baby has its own unique fingerprints and toe prints.

From Riches to Rags

Read Job 1:20–22; 2:10–11; 42:1–6, 10–17

"Naked I came from my mother's womb,
and naked I will depart.
The LORD gave and the LORD has taken away;
may the name of the LORD be praised." (1:21)

Job was a man who had it all. He had great wealth and a big, happy family. He loved the Lord, and every day was a like a dream come true. He was living the perfect life. One day tragedy struck out of the blue. His children were killed and his wealth vanished all in the same day. To make matters worse, he became afflicted with a disease that covered his body in painful sores. His wife and friends mocked him. He was in a seemingly hopeless situation. In fact, Job said he wished he had not been born. Yet he refused to blame God. Through all of his misery, he still trusted in God. In the end, the Lord restored his health and his wealth and even gave him more children.

Life is not always easy. In fact, it can be extremely difficult and painful. Even in the most difficult of situations, God is there watching over you. He loves you, and you can trust him.

Lord, you know what I am facing in my life. I can't do it without you. Help me, Lord. Amen.

Write a prayer to God thanking him for always being there even when you can't feel his presence. Ask him to give you the answers you need.

Unexplainable Peace

Read John 14:25–31

"Peace I leave with you; my peace I give you. . . . Do not let your hearts be troubled and do not be afraid." (v. 27)

Jesus was talking to his closest followers, his disciples, and telling them that he was going to be leaving them; he was returning to heaven. He told them not to worry because he was sending the Holy Spirit to them. The Holy Spirit lives inside of Christians, those who have trusted Christ for salvation. If you are a Christian, you have the Holy Spirit living in you. The job of the Holy Spirit is to guide you and comfort you. Do you need guidance? Do you need comfort? You can turn to the Holy Spirit, who is God, to give you peace. This peace that comes from God is different from the world's peace. God's peace can be found in all circumstances. Even when times are tough, God can give you a peace that passes understanding. Regardless of your circumstances, you do not need to fear. Trust God instead.

Dear Father, thank you for sending the Holy Spirit to comfort me. Guide me as I make decisions for myself and my baby. Amen.

What decisions are you facing? What threatens to steal your peace?
Tell God about it.

20 **WEEKS:** The fetus is now about ten inches long from head to heel and weighs eleven ounces. The baby has unique waking and sleeping patterns and even has a favorite position to sleep in. The pregnancy is about half over, and the mother is beginning to "show." Studies indicate that babies can feel pain at twenty weeks and possibly even earlier.

You Are God's Friend

Read John 15:9–17

"I have told you this so that my joy may be in you and that your joy may be complete." (v. 11)

This is an exciting time in your pregnancy. You recently found out or will soon find out that your baby is a boy or a girl. You can begin to pick out names for your baby and plan how you will decorate for him or her and what he or she will wear!

This passage talks about love and joy and friendship, all things that will be important in your baby's life. In this passage, we learn that Jesus calls us friends and that he wants us to have complete joy. He also tells us to love each other. Living a life of love and joy is what the Christian life is all about. You can look forward to sharing love and joy and friendship with your child.

So today, you can rejoice and show God's love to someone who needs it. You have a lot to celebrate!

Father, I thank you that you call me friend. It is a great privilege to be a friend of God. In Jesus' name, amen.

Write about love, joy, and friendship in your life. What brings you joy? Who has been a friend to you? Who has shown you love, and how have they shown it? How will you show love to your baby?

Legacy of Love

Read Deuteronomy 5:1–22

*"But showing love to a thousand generations of those who
love me and keep my commandments."* (v. 10)

The Lord told Moses to go to the top of Mt. Sinai, and there
he gave him the Ten Commandments. These were rules for living.
These rules tell us not to kill or steal or cheat or lie or swear or be
jealous. They also tell us to honor our parents, to set aside a day
to worship God and to worship only God. When we keep these
commandments, we live in peace. Can you imagine what life
would be like if no one cheated or stole or lied? Imagine a world
where everyone loved God and honored their parents.

We can't control the world, or even any other person, but
we do make choices about our own lives. This passage gives us
a promise not only for ourselves, but for our children. God says
he will show love to those who keep his commandments and to
a thousand generations. This means that as you follow and obey
God, you are ensuring God's love for your children and grandchildren and descendants for many generations to come.

Thank you, Father, for your love. Help me to follow you.
In Jesus' name, amen.

Which commandments are you keeping? Which are hard for you to keep? How does it make you feel to know that your obedience will affect your children and grandchildren in the future?

22 **WEEKS:** The baby is about eleven inches long and weighs about one pound. If the baby is male, his testicles are beginning to descend from the abdomen to the scrotum. Hair is visible on his or her head and body. From now until about thirty-two weeks, the baby feels pain more intensely than at any other time in development.

Counting Hairs

Read Matthew 10:29–31

"And even the very hairs of your head are all numbered." (v. 30)

You may be thinking about hair these days. Your hair may be thicker and more luxurious with your pregnancy. Or maybe your hair is thinning and every day seems like a bad hair day. You have probably wondered if your baby will born with a headful of hair or will be bald. Will his hair be curly or straight, blond or brunette? Will his hair look like mine or his grandfather's?

One thing we know for sure is that God knows exactly what your baby will look like and he has designed your baby just right. He has also designed you perfectly. The Bible says he numbers the hairs on your head. Incredible to think about, isn't it? The number of hairs on your head is ever changing, yet God always knows exactly how many there are. Do you know why? Because he loves you that much! Even as a doting mother, you won't count your baby's hairs, but God will. He cares about each and every detail of your life, even the things that may seem unimportant to you. Nothing about you is unimportant to God. He knows everything about you, and he loves you despite all of your flaws.

The very next thing Jesus says, after stating that the hairs on your head are numbered, is "so don't be afraid." Circumstances in our lives may surprise us, but they don't surprise God. He is watching over every aspect of our lives, so have no reason to fear. Trust him today.

> Lord, thank you that you watch over every detail of my life. Help me to remember how tenderly you care for me. Help me not to be afraid. Amen.

How do you picture the next few years with your baby? What are you excited about? What are you nervous about?

Faith that Heals

Read Luke 8:42–47

*She came up behind him and touched the edge of his cloak,
and immediately her bleeding stopped.* (v. 44)

Jesus was walking down the road, and the crowds of people who wanted to get to him almost crushed him. Think mosh pit on steroids. They knew that he had the power to heal, and they wanted to be healed. They knew they were needy, and they believed Jesus could meet their needs. At least they hoped so. One of these people was a woman who had been bleeding for twelve years. Imagine bleeding for twelve years! She came close to Jesus and touched his clothing from behind and her bleeding stopped that instant! Jesus knew it and asked who had touched him. His disciples were confused by the question because many people were crowded around him, pressing into him. But Jesus knew that this woman was different. She touched him believing that he would heal her. Jesus found her and told her that her faith had healed her.

Dear God, I believe that you have the power to heal my body and my heart. I need your touch today. Amen.

What do you need Jesus to heal in your life? Do you have broken relationships, broken dreams, a broken heart? Write about the things you believe Jesus can heal.

24 **WEEKS:** The baby now weighs approximately 1½ pounds and inhales amniotic fluid in preparation for breathing. The ear has developed to the point where the baby recognizes his or her mother's voice, breathing and heartbeat. About a week ago, rapid eye movements began, an activity associated with dreaming. The baby may have a blink-startle response resulting from sound applied to the mother's abdomen. Some babies born at this stage of development are able to survive.

God Who Hears

Read Psalm 116

I love the LORD, for he heard my voice; he heard my cry for mercy. Because he turned his ear to me, I will call on him as long as I live. (vv. 1–2)

Even now your baby can hear your voice and she recognizes it. You are her mother, and her ear is tuned in to your voice. As a mother, you will spend countless hours listening to your child. She will come to you for comfort and wisdom, for love and approval, for advice and help. She will sometimes be angry and will resist what you are saying to her. But you will always listen.

The Lord has his ear turned to you. He knows your deepest needs and desires. Psalm 116 talks about a person who has been overcome by trouble and sorrow, a person in great need, a person who needs to be rescued. He was stumbling, crying, fearing death. He could not save himself, so he did the only thing he could do, he cried out for God to save him. And God heard his cry. He had discovered that people had lied to him and could not be trusted. But the Lord was faithful to him. The Lord freed him from his chains and gave him peace and rest. He will do the same thing for you. Your baby is not the only one who hears your every word. God hears your every word and every thought. His ear is turned to you. He is waiting to rescue you from whatever has held you captive. Speak to him today. Let the healing begin.

Father, you know the things that threaten my sense of peace. You know the things that cause me to stumble and to cry. You know the people who have hurt me. Thank you for hearing my cry. Free me from my chains. I trust you. Amen.

Tell the Lord the things that entangle you. Tell him what hurts your heart and causes you to stumble and fall. Let him heal the places that are hurt and lift you up so you can sing his praise.

Who Is This Guy?

Read Matthew 8:23–27

The men were amazed and asked, "What kind of man is this? Even the winds and the waves obey him!" (v. 27)

Jesus was out on a boat with his disciples, taking a much-needed nap. While he was sleeping, a huge storm came on the lake. The disciples panicked, believing they were going to drown. They were terrified when they woke Jesus up. Jesus told the wind and waves to stop causing trouble, and you guessed it, they did. Jesus asked the disciples why they were so afraid. It didn't make sense for them to be so fearful; Jesus was right there with them. We are the same way sometimes. We panic when things don't go as we have planned. Instead of calmly turning to Jesus, we are terrified. Even though we can't see him like the disciples could, Jesus is right beside us too. He will calm the storms in our lives as well.

Dear God, help me not to panic when trouble comes into my life. Help me to calmly trust you to take care of me. Thank you for your faithfulness. In Jesus' name, amen.

What storms are you facing now? Are you panicking or trusting?
Tell Jesus about the storm and trust him to calm it.

26 **WEEKS:** Now the baby weighs almost two pounds, and he or she can react to sounds outside the mother's body. Eyes can now respond to light, and the permanent teeth buds are apparent in the gums. Eyelashes and eyebrows are well formed, and the hair on the baby's head is growing longer.

A Loving Father

Read Luke 15:11–32

"But we had to celebrate and be glad, because this brother of yours was dead and is alive again; he was lost and is found." (v. 32)

Once upon a time there lived a rich man who had two sons. The oldest son was obedient and helped his father to manage the family business. The youngest son was spoiled and demanded his inheritance while his father was still alive. He took his undeserved money and spent it on wild living. He found himself homeless and hungry. He decided to return to his father and ask him to hire him so that he would not starve to death. While he was still a long way from home, his father saw him and told his servants to prepare a huge celebration for the return of his son.

Jesus tells us this story because he is painting a picture of our heavenly Father, who is always watching and waiting for us to return to him. He is always ready to forgive us and to welcome us into his family.

Dear God, thank you for your forgiveness and your love for me. Amen.

Are you running from God? Do you know someone who is? Write about how you feel about returning to your Father or who you can help to return to God.

Gratitude

Read Luke 17:11–17

*One of them, when he saw he was healed, came
back, praising God in a loud voice.* (v. 15)

Leprosy is a highly contagious, debilitating disease. It is
characterized by sores on the body that spread, causing paralysis,
wasting of muscle, and producing deformities. It can be cured
by antibiotics, but in Jesus' day there was no known cure. People
with leprosy, lepers, were sent away to live in leper colonies so
that they would not spread the disease.

One day, ten lepers approached Jesus, asking him to heal
them. He was their only hope. He spoke to them, and as they
walked, they were healed. One of them ran back to Jesus to thank
him when he saw that he was well. He threw himself at Jesus' feet
and praised God in a loud voice. He was truly grateful for what
God had done for him.

Thank you, Father, that you are a God of miracles. Help me
not to forget to thank you for all you have done for me.
Amen.

What has Jesus done for you? Have you thanked him? Take time today to thank God for your baby and other blessings in your life.

28 **WEEKS:** The baby is now approximately fifteen inches long and weighs about 2½ pounds. With the support of intensive care, a baby born at this stage is capable of breathing air. The brain is developed enough to coordinate rhythmic breathing and regulate body temperature. As the baby continues to gain weight, the skin becomes less wrinkled and more smooth.

No Swollen Feet

Read Nehemiah 9:13–21

"But you are a forgiving God, gracious and compassionate, slow to anger and abounding in love. Therefore you did not desert them." (v. 17)

God had rescued his people from slavery. He sent Moses to free them through a series of miracles, and yet they quickly turned their backs on him. Almost immediately after God set them free, his people began to worship other gods. This passage tells about how even after the Israelites turned their backs on God, he continued to care for them. He sent them a cloud to guide them each day as they were in the desert for forty years and a fire to guide them at night so they would not get lost. He sent them food (manna) directly from heaven so they would not go hungry. He even took care to see that their feet would not swell as they walked. He was loving and compassionate toward them even as they continued to rebel against him.

This is the God of the universe! His goodness is not dependent on our behavior. Maybe you are in a spiritual desert yourself. Maybe you are rebelling against God, choosing to do things your way instead of his. He has not abandoned you. He is slow to anger and abounding in love, caring for you even in your rebellion, whether it is big or small. Will you turn to him today?

> Lord, I thank you that you love me even when I am unlovable. I pray that you would change my heart to be like yours. I want to follow you, not fight you. Thank you for your forgiveness, compassion and love. Amen.

In what areas of your life have you rebelled? How have you seen God's care even in the midst of rebellion? Write a prayer of confession and thankfulness.

What Are You Wearing?

Read Colossians 3:12–14

Therefore, as God's chosen people, holy and dearly loved, clothe yourselves with compassion, kindness, humility, gentleness and patience. (v. 12)

These days it may be difficult to find something to wear. Your body is changing rapidly, and you hardly recognize yourself in the mirror. You sometimes wonder if your body will ever be the same again. Now is a good time to think about what God wants us to put on. He tells us to clothe ourselves with his characteristics. This means that that stuff does not come naturally to us. We have to put it on. In ourselves we can be selfish, unkind and impatient. It is very easy for us to focus on ourselves, our circumstances and our problems, especially when we are pregnant, because we do have a lot to deal with! But we have another choice. We can choose to look outside of ourselves and to focus on the needs and well-being of those around us (or inside of us). We can be gentle and patient even with those who are not kind to us, those who mistreat us. We can choose to see people through God's eyes of compassion and love. Because God has forgiven us, we can choose to forgive others. We can put the needs of others before our own needs because we know that God will take care of us. We can trust God to take care of us, and that frees us to take better care of others.

Father, thank you that I can clothe myself with your goodness. I want to be a woman who puts on compassion and kindness and gentleness. I confess that this is not naturally who I am, but who I want to be in you. Help me to be the woman you created me to be. Amen.

What will you wear today? Picture yourself putting on each of the characteristics listed in the verse above. What will they look like on you?

God Will Answer

Read Luke 18:1–8

"And will not God bring about justice for his chosen ones, who cry out to him day and night? Will he keep putting them off? I tell you, he will see that they get justice, and quickly." (vv. 7–8)

Jesus tells a story of a judge who didn't fear God and didn't care about people. He was a bad guy who had a position of power and authority. You may know someone like that. In this town where the judge was making decisions also lived a widow who needed the judge's help. He, of course, had no desire to help her because he didn't care what happened to her and he had no interest in doing the right thing. Nevertheless, the widow kept going to the judge asking for him to grant her justice against her adversary. He refused her time and again, but she refused to give up. She continued to plead with him for justice. Eventually, the judge gave her what she wanted so she would go away and leave him alone.

The Bible says this story is a lesson on prayer for us. It is an example of how God wants us to come to him with our needs and requests. The Bible says we should always pray and not give up. The Bible is not comparing God to the heartless judge. It is showing us that if this heartless judge will grant justice, imagine how much more our loving God longs to answer our prayers! Don't be afraid to go to God again and again with your requests. Do not think that he tires of hearing them. He gives us this story to remind us that he wants us to always come to him and that he will answer.

> Thank you, Lord, for listening to my prayers and for answering them. Help me to remember to always pray and not give up. In Jesus' name, amen.

What are your deepest needs and desires? Tell them to God now.

Walking on Water

Read Matthew 14:22–32

*Then Peter got down out of the boat, walked on
the water and came toward Jesus.* (v. 29)

When we think of walking on water, we usually picture Jesus
doing the walking. Jesus did walk on water, but the Bible tells
us that Peter did too. Now Peter was just an ordinary person
like you and me. He got angry, he told lies, and he even denied
knowing Jesus more than once to save his own skin. He was by
no means perfect. But when Peter had his eyes on Jesus, he was
able to walk on water. This story takes place during the middle
of the night when the disciples see Jesus walking on the lake.
They are afraid thinking they see a ghost. Jesus calls out to them
identifying himself and telling them not to be afraid. Peter says,
"Lord, if it's you, tell me to come to you on the water." Jesus says,
"Come." And Peter walks on the water just like Jesus, not because
Peter is special, but because he has faith in Jesus. Jesus told him to
go and he went. The story goes on to say that when Peter saw the
wind, he was afraid and began to sink. Immediately Jesus rescued
him. This story contains lessons for us. When we keep our eyes
on Jesus, we can do the impossible. When we doubt, we begin to
sink but even then Jesus will rescue us.

Lord, help me to keep my eyes on you. Don't let me look at the troubles around me, but only on you who will rescue me and keep me safe. I love you. Amen.

What is Jesus calling you to do? Is he telling you to get out the boat and come to him? Will you keep your eyes on Jesus and do what he is telling you to do?

No Lunch for the Lions

Read Daniel 6

The king was overjoyed and gave orders to lift Daniel out of the den. And when Daniel was lifted from the den, no wound was found on him, because he had trusted in his God. (v. 23)

The king of Babylon was very impressed with Daniel, who was a man of God. He was so impressed that he had decided to put Daniel in charge of the whole kingdom. As you might have guessed, this made the other rulers very jealous of Daniel. So they devised a plan to destroy Daniel. They knew that Daniel prayed publicly every day, and so they suggested to the king that he make a rule that anyone who prayed to anyone other than the king be put into a den of lions to be eaten. Because the king was a very prideful man, he issued this decree of the death penalty for anyone who prayed to anyone other than himself. Because Daniel loved and trusted God, he continued to pray to him each day without fear, even after this law was put into effect. The jealous rulers brought this to the attention of the king, and the king reluctantly sent Daniel to the den of hungry lions. God closed the mouths of the fierce creatures, and Daniel emerged without a scratch!

Our God is powerful. Do not be afraid to trust him to take care of you.

Dear God, you are amazing. Thank you for rescuing Daniel. Help me to be faithful as he was. Amen.

Are you facing jealousy? Are others mistreating you? What did you learn from this story?

_____

_____

_____

_____

_____

_____

_____

_____

_____

_____

_____

_____

_____

_____

_____

_____

Beautiful Feet

Read Romans 10:13–15

"How beautiful are the feet of those who bring good news!" (v. 15)

You have probably thought some about your baby's feet. Baby feet are so soft and sweet and tickle-able! You will spend many hours washing and tickling and playing "this little piggy" with your baby.

The Bible has something to say about our feet. The Bible says our feet are beautiful if we bring the good news. The good news is that "everyone who calls on the name of the Lord will be saved." Salvation is found in Jesus Christ, God's Son who died for us. He died for our sins and rose from the dead. We receive eternal life through faith in Jesus Christ. We can live with God forever when we trust Jesus. It's that simple! God asks us to trust his Son to save us, and then he tells us to tell others this good news. This passage reminds us that people won't know unless we tell them. So if you have never trusted Jesus as your Savior, trust him now. If you are already a child of God, you need to make your feet beautiful by telling others about the free gift of salvation.

Lord, I thank you for salvation in Jesus Christ. I know that I am a sinner and need you to save me. I believe that Jesus died on the cross for me and that he rose from the dead. I trust in Jesus to save me. Help me to tell others about what Jesus has done for me and for them. Help me to have beautiful feet. Amen.

Who do you know who needs to hear the good news of salvation through Jesus Christ? When will you tell them?

34 **WEEKS:** The baby is now about seventeen inches long, weighs 4½ pounds and continues to grow and mature. By this stage of development, the eyes are wide open, and if a light were shone into them, the pupils would constrict. The head is covered in hair, the fingernails have reached the tips of the fingers and the toenails are close behind. The lungs are still developing, so if born at this stage, the baby will probably need some assistance breathing.

Mighty Children

Read Psalm 112

Blessed are those who fear the Lord, who find great delight in his commands. Their children will be mighty in the land; the generation of the upright will be blessed. (vv. 1–2)

This passage describes a person who fears the Lord. This is a person who sees God for who he is and therefore honors and respects him. This person delights in his commands. She loves to honor and obey her God. She is generous and fair and compassionate. She is fearless because she trusts her God to take care of her in all circumstances. She is not afraid to share what she has with others because she knows God will provide for her.

The Bible says good things will come to this person. She will triumph over her enemies. She will be remembered forever. God promises blessings for her children as well. Her children will be strong, and they will be blessed.

If you love to honor and obey God, your children will be blessed. Your fear of the Lord will bring blessings to your children. It's a promise.

Lord, thank you for the promise of blessing my children as I fear you and delight in your commands. Draw me close to you. Help me walk in your ways. I am so thankful to be able to bring blessings to my child through my actions. Teach me how. Amen.

Do you love to obey God's commands? Are there any commands that you struggle to obey? Tell the Lord about how you want to serve him and where you need his help to be obedient.

Love Never Fails

Read 1 Corinthians 13

Love is patient, love is kind. . . . Love does not delight in evil but rejoices with the truth. It always protects, always trusts, always hopes, always perseveres. Love never fails. (vv. 4, 6–8)

Have you ever been let down by someone who was supposed to love you? Has anyone ever told you he would love you forever and it turned out to be a lie? Everyone wants to be loved forever by someone who will never let you down. The Bible talks about this type of love. This love is patient and kind and does not keep track of our failures. This love protects, trusts, never gives up. This love does not get angry easily and is not rude. This is a perfect love. It is God's love. God's love does not require perfection from us. It is love that never gives up no matter how many times we fail. People will always let you down, even the best of people. You are safe with God. He knows the worst things you have ever done. He knows your darkest thoughts, and he loves you still. You are precious to him.

Dear God, thank you for loving me so much. Help me to remember how much you love me and to be loving to the people in my life. In Jesus' name, amen.

Write about what it means to love someone the way God loves. Describe a perfect loving relationship. How will you show love to your child?

Nesting

Read Psalm 84

*Even the sparrow has found a home, and the swallow a nest
for herself, where she may have her young—a place near your
altar, L*ORD *Almighty, my King and my God.* (v. 3)

You are getting close to the birth of your baby. Your mind is
probably racing with many emotions, and you may be very tired.
One thing that many women experience as the birth draws near
is something called the "nesting instinct." Many women report
a burst of energy, causing them to clean the house and get the
nursery prepared for baby's arrival. It is called the nesting instinct
because this preparation for baby is being compared to a mother
bird making a nest as a place to care for her babies.

The Bible says that God is preparing a place for his children
too. Heaven is a place of great joy. In heaven there will be no suf-
fering, no hunger, no thirst, no tears (Revelation 7:16–17). Just as
you are planning and preparing a beautiful place for your child,
God is preparing a beautiful, safe place for you. Jesus said, *"In my
Father's house are many rooms; if it were not so I would have told
you. I am going there to prepare a place for you. And if I go and
prepare a place for you, I will come back and take you to be with
me that you also may be where I am"* (John 14:2–3). If you have

trusted in Jesus Christ to save you, you have a home, a beautiful home, waiting for you in heaven!

> O Lord, I am so thankful for my home in heaven and for my home on earth. Please help me make my home a safe and happy place for my baby. Help me also to teach my child about our home in heaven. In Jesus' name, amen.

Write about all the preparations you are making for the arrival of your baby.

Small Spark, Big Fire

Read James 3:2–12

Likewise, the tongue is a small part of the body, but it makes great boasts. Consider what a great forest is set on fire by a small spark. (v. 5)

Fires are extremely destructive. Fires cause loss of property and even life every day. Often a fire is started by an innocent mistake: someone falls asleep while smoking, knocks over a candle, leaves something burning on the stove. What begins as a careless act ends in great loss. Sometimes fires are set with malicious intent. The person seeks to destroy, and fire is his method of choice.

The Bible compares our tongues to fire. We can destroy quickly using our tongues. A careless word can cause unseen damage. Most of us can remember hurtful things that were said to us with seemingly little thought, yet the words are played back in our minds for years to come. We also remember malicious things said to us in anger. Words are powerful weapons. When someone stabs us in the back, words are usually the knife.

Take great care with your words, especially now with the imminent birth of your child. Your little one will be listening to everything that you say for years to come. Use your words to tell him that you love him and that God loves him. Use your words to teach him to serve the God who loves him. Bless him with your mouth.

Father, I confess that my words are not always pleasing to you. Help me to learn to be careful in my speech and to use my words to bless, not to curse. In Jesus' name, amen.

How have you misused words? Gossip? Lies? Cursing? Anger? Is there someone you need to ask for forgiveness? How will you use your words to bless your child and others?

Due Date

Read Luke 2:1–20

While they were there, the time came for the baby to be born. (v. 6)

Mary was pregnant with God's Son Jesus and was fast approaching her due date. She was surely full of emotions, just as you are. Maybe her back hurt, and she was probably very tired. But a decree had been issued that required her to travel a long distance to Bethlehem to register for a census. She probably had to travel many miles on the back of a donkey. Sounds very unpleasant for a woman at the end of her pregnancy, doesn't it? This was the law, however, so Mary made the journey. While she was there, just as God had planned, Jesus was born. Mary gave birth to God's own Son who had come to save us from our sins. What a blessed event!

You are preparing now for your own blessed event. Although your child will not save the world from sin, God has a great plan for him. He planned your child's life before the foundation of the world, and he chose you to be his mother. You are chosen, honored, and privileged to be the one to raise this child to be the person God has created him to be. The Lord gave you this task, and he will give you everything you need to accomplish it. Look to him, and he will guide you.

Lord, I thank you for giving me this child. I pray that you will help me to raise him to honor and serve you. Thank you for saving me. Amen.

Write about how you think Mary felt as she gave birth to Jesus that night. How do you feel about giving birth soon?

Beginnings

Read Romans 12:1–2

Do not conform any longer to the pattern of this world, but be transformed by the renewing of your mind. Then you will be able to test and approve what God's will is—his good, pleasing and perfect will. (v. 2)

We all love new beginnings. Many of us celebrate on New Year's Eve because we are looking for a new beginning, a chance to begin again. New beginnings bring hope and promise. Regardless of what has happened in the past, we can start afresh. We look with hope to the future because we believe things can and will get better.

The birth of a child is a time of tremendous joy and hope. As you look into the eyes of your child, you see all the beautiful things that are yet to come. New birth is full of promise. Your child will see the things you have seen with new eyes, and she will see things you have never seen. You will experience life again, through her eyes.

In Jesus, there is always hope and promise. God promises us not only change, but transformation. He changes us completely when we trust Christ as Savior. The Bible even calls it being born again. He promises transformation. Just as he changes an ugly caterpillar to a beautiful butterfly, he takes what is ugly and broken in our lives and replaces it with joy and peace.

Lord, I thank you for eternal life in Christ and for the life of my child. I thank you for new beginnings and that your mercy is new every day. I love you. Amen.

What are some things you are looking forward to experiencing through your child's eyes?

40 **WEEKS:** The baby is now around twenty inches long and may weigh seven to eight pounds. He or she has a plump body and a firm grasp. Typically, the baby is head down in the mother's pelvis and awaiting birth.

Feeding Time

Read 2 Timothy 3:10–17

And how from infancy you have known the Holy Scriptures, which are able to make you wise for salvation through faith in Christ Jesus. (v. 15)

It seems like newborns eat all the time. Whether you are nursing or bottle-feeding, you feel like you are constantly feeding your baby. Just about the time you think you will have a minute to yourself to shower or relax or get a bite to eat, your baby is crying, asking to be fed yet again. It seems he can never get enough; his hunger is insatiable.

God created your baby to eat frequently because he is growing so fast. He needs food so that he will grow and develop properly. Feeding your baby also serves another purpose. It gives you time to be together. When you feed your baby, you are meeting her needs, and this develops the bond of trust that will last a lifetime. She is hungry, and you take her in your arms and give her exactly what she needs. She quickly learns that she is not alone and that you are there to meet her needs. She is safe in your care.

You are also safe in the arms of Jesus. God says his Word is like food for our souls. We need to read God's Word, the Bible, so that we can stay healthy and strong. The Bible gives us the strength we need to do the work he has called us to do. Even in these busy days of caring for your baby, don't forget to feed your spirit too by reading God's Word. Read it out loud sometimes. Your baby will love it too!

> Lord, you are good and your mercy endures forever. Thank you for your Word, your Son, and my child. Amen.

What is your favorite part of the Bible? Write about how you will tell your child about what God has done for you.

Dear Friend...

Thank you for allowing me to share in a part of this special time of your life. I am so grateful to God and to you for allowing me to be a part of your journey. God could have chosen anyone to parent your child, and he chose you. God never makes mistakes, so you can be sure that you are right person for the job. Keep looking to him, and he will continue to guide you.

With love,
Melissa

A Prayer for You

Father, thank you so much for this mother and this child. I pray that you will bless this mother with courage and grace and wisdom to raise her child to know and love you. I thank you that you will give her everything she needs to be the mother her baby needs. I pray that you will bring godly people into her life to help support her and guide her. I pray your richest blessings on this baby. I pray that this child will be healthy and strong and will come to know you and your love at a very young age. Bless this family beyond their wildest dreams! In Jesus' precious name, amen.

Read Psalm 139: "I praise you because I am fearfully and won-
derfully made; your works are wonderful, I know that full well"
(v. 14). Write a letter to your child about her birthday. Tell her
how you feel and your dreams for her.

"Forget the former things; do not dwell on the past. See, I am doing a new thing! Now it springs up; do you not perceive it? I am making a way in the wilderness and streams in the wasteland" (Isaiah 43:18–19). *You are beginning a whole new phase in your life! Reflect on how you have changed in the past year and the new things you are excited about.*

"And Jesus grew in wisdom and stature, and in favor with God and man" (Luke 2:52). You and your baby will grow and change together. How will you teach him about Jesus?

"And let us consider how we may spur one another on toward love and good deeds, not giving up meeting together, as some are in the habit of doing, but encouraging one another—and all the more as you see the Day approaching" (Hebrews 10:24–25). God does not want you to live your life alone. Look for a Bible-teaching church where you feel comfortable, a Bible study, or a mothers' group. List places you can contact.

Read Joshua 4:1–7. In this story, the Jews saved stones as memorials to teach their children about what God had done for them. What do you want to tell your child about how God has taken care of you? How will you remember to tell her?

"As a mother comforts her child, so will I comfort you; and you will be comforted over Jerusalem" (Isaiah 66:13). Write about God's love and comfort for you. If you would like to continue with reading the Bible and journaling your thoughts weekly as a new mother, you may want to use A Mother's Comfort, *a journal for your baby's first year.*

_____

_____

_____

_____

_____

_____

_____

_____

_____

_____

_____

_____

_____

_____

_____

_____

_____

_____